# CREATURES OF DARKNESS

# CREATURES
## OF

# DARKNESS

## By John F. Waters
## Illustrated by
## Harriett Springer

**WALKER AND COMPANY**
**NEW YORK**

First published in the United States of America
in 1975 by the Walker Publishing Company, Inc.

Published simultaneously in Canada
by Fitzhenry & Whiteside, Limited, Toronto.

Trade ISBN: 0–8027–6199–2
Reinf ISBN: 0–8027–6200–X

Library of Congress Catalog Card Number: 74–78113

Printed in the United States of America.

Designed by Robert Bartosiewicz

10 9 8 7 6 5 4 3 2 1

# CONTENTS

# INTRODUCTION

Animals live just about anywhere in the world. They live in oceans and lakes, dry deserts and high mountains. They live on rocks and under logs, inside things and on top of things. They even live where it is dark all the time.

Everyone knows what darkness is. It is having little or no light. It could be in a room closet with the door closed. That is dark. It could be down in the cellar or up in the attic with the lights out. It could be outside on a moonless night. That's dark. Under the bed covers it is very dark too.

Many different kinds of animals live where it is dark. Some have huge eyes that reflect what little light there is. Others have no eyes but have extremely sensitive senses of touch, taste and hearing. Some respond to vibrations in water. Some, like bats, can tell where objects are by listening to sound echoes. Animals that live in darkness have these special "adaptations" which make it possible for them to find food and live long enough to produce offspring that have these same adaptations.

# CREATURES
# OF
# DARKNESS

WHITE CRAYFISH

# 1 CREATURES OF A CAVE

In a cave it is always dark. There is never any light except at the entrance. The temperature is always cool. It never gets hot. There are no changing seasons of the year in a cave. There is no weather. The wind doesn't blow. There are no rainstorms or windstorms, no hail, and never any snow.

Deep inside a dark cave it is also fairly quiet. There are no noises such as leaves fluttering in the trees or animals running around in tall grasses hunting for food. There are no sounds of insects making their night noises, nor the musical sounds of birds calling out from trees or porch roofs. The few sounds in a cave are made by an occasional drop of water splashing in a pool or the squeal of a bat as it flaps its wings while leaving or returning from a feeding trip.

Because there is no sunlight there are no green plants living inside a cave. Without green plants there is not much food. Cave creatures are constantly searching for the little bit of food that is there.

Green plants are still important to cave animals. Green plants outside a cave supply food to the animals inside. Food is brought in. Bats live in caves during the day, then fly out at night to find food. They eat insects that feed on green plants and the fruit of plants. As they hang upside down on cave ceilings they drop their wastes on the cave floor. These wastes are food for small cave creatures such as snails, beetles, and microscopic bacteria.

Sometimes an outside animal drops into a cave through an opening in the ground. If the animal cannot get out it dies and its body is food for other creatures. When a cave animal dies it doesn't last very long. Because of the shortage of food other animals immediately eat it.

Flood waters bring food into a cave. It may rain a lot and then water seeps in through the ground and through holes in the roof bringing in bits of food. Wandering animals such as raccoons may visit a cave and leave behind wastes that become food for animals. Pack rats and birds, such as owls and wrens, may visit a cave and build nests. They go outside to feed and sometimes bring in food and leave wastes.

There are three groups of cave animals: *Troglobites* means cave dwellers. Most of them have undeveloped eyes or no eyes at all. They usually have no color and are true cave animals in the sense that they could not live any place else.

*Trogloxenes* are cave guests. They move in and out of a cave, usually looking for food. Examples are crickets, bats, mosquitoes, and some kinds of birds, mice, and rats. At one time this group included man, since early man lived in caves. Now, however, only a few tribes in isolated parts of the world are cave dwellers.

*Troglophiles* means cave lovers. They are animals that may live in a cave but do not necessarily have to do so. Examples of such animals are salamanders, beetles, and earthworms.

## TROGLOBITES

Because there is no light, eyes are not important to most cave animals. A few cave creatures have eyes that can see, others have eyes that cannot see, or they have nothing where eyes used to be. Fatty lumps are in place of eyes on blind fish that live in pools deep within caves. Eyeless fish are the most well-known of the true cave creatures of darkness.

When the first eyeless cave fish was found in the United States in 1842 it was quite an event. Because it was colorless and had no eyes people became curious and collected specimens to take home. Due to the collecting there are few of these cave fish left in caves today.

All cave fish have special ways to live in the darkness. They have better senses outside of their eyes than other fish. On the top and sides of the head and near the jaws are sensory nerves. These nerves allow the fish to feel other animals close to them. Cave fish also have a good sense of smell and can detect very faint odors in the water. Many cave fish have a lateral line system. This means they have a line of sensitive cells running along the sides of their body, similar to that of surface fish that live in lakes, rivers, and the sea. Animals with a lateral line system can find prey in the darkness by picking up their presence through vibrations in the

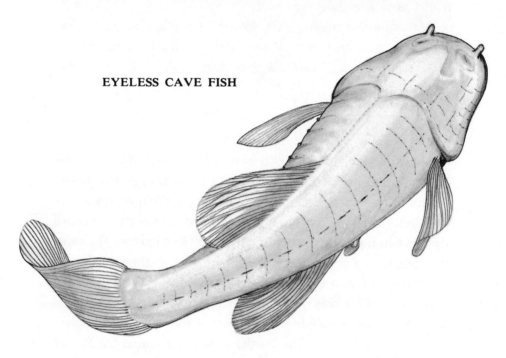

EYELESS CAVE FISH

water. They also have longer fins that enable them to swim with long gliding movements that do not interfere with their ability to detect vibrations. Blind fish may actually find their food more easily than fish that can see.

The white crayfish is also blind. It has eyes just like its outside relative, the freshwater crayfish, but it cannot see. Some crayfish live in shallow pools, while others live in water that is deep.

Cave salamanders are another kind of troglobite. They differ from their relatives that live above ground in that they have smaller eyes or no eyes at all, a thin body, flat snout, long legs, and no color. Some are almost transparent and one can see their blood vessels inside their skin.

With long legs the cave salamander is able to move through the water easily as it hunts for food. When it does eat, the troglobitic salamander digests its food very well and its body uses it carefully. Therefore the salamander can live a long time with little or no food. In an experiment one salamander stayed alive in a laboratory for four years without food.

There is one strange blind salamander that at one stage of its life cycle has sight. When it is in the early stages of its life, the larva form that lives in water has eyes that see. But then as it grows, its eyelids overlap and come together. Then the inside of the eye breaks down and it becomes blind.

CAVE SALAMANDER

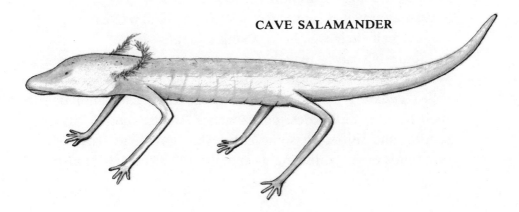

In the United States scientists have found about 400 different kinds of creatures that live permanently in caves. But many of them are flatworms, bacteria, and beetles, of which scientists know very little. The reason is simple. First, not all caves are big enough for man to enter. There are long, tiny passages, small openings, and little streams that are difficult to trace. These tiny places make it hard for scientists to discover what animals are there and how they live.

Scientists are not sure why some troglobites are blind. Did they lose their eyes and sight through many years of living in a cave? Or were the ancestors of the blind animals becoming blind before they moved to caves? If they were blind to begin with, their chances of surviving were much better in a dark cave than in the outside world.

## TROGLOXENES

One of the best-known trogloxene animals is the bat. Bats are the main source of food for all of the other animals that live in a cave. At dusk they leave after spending the day inside the cave hanging upside down from the roof. They fly through the night searching for food such as insects or fruit. They may travel as far as 50 miles to find enough to eat; they can eat half their weight in a single night.

Some big caves may have as many as a million bats. Wastes from the bats drop to the cave floor. Their waste is called *guano*. It has food value for the other cave animals such as lice, millipedes, cockroaches, snails, moths, cave beetles, and mites. In some caves that have had bats for thousands of years, the guano may be 100 feet thick. It also

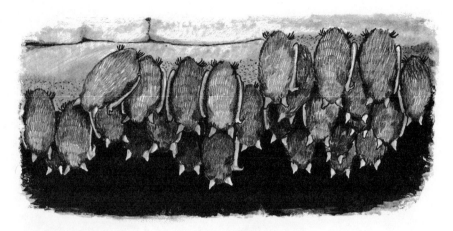

BATS AT REST

gets washed into underground pools and streams, where it feeds fish, flatworms, and crawfish.

Bats themselves are food for other cave animals. Dead bat carcasses end up on the floor; baby bats may lose their grip on their mother and fall to their deaths. Then beetles, ticks, and other insects feed on them.

Despite superstitions and tales, bats are not frightening creatures. They are merely peculiar looking. They are mammals since they have fur and give birth to baby bats that are nursed on milk.

Another common trogloxene is the cave rat. It is a clean animal, pale brown in color with dark brown eyes. It lives in caves during the day and forages at night. The cave rat brings back such things as bright bits of ribbon, stone, pieces of glass, tin, and anything else that attracts its eye and can be carried.

CAVE RAT

Cave crickets are seen as often as bats. Most cave crickets live near the cave entrance so they can be near their food supply on the outside. They are two inches long or less, light tan in color and have long antennae and long rear legs. Unlike crickets that live outside of caves, cave crickets don't chirp. One kind is believed to be troglobitic—never leaving the cave.

Most cave crickets have the same routine as bats and

cave rats in that they go outside at night to find food and then return in the morning before it gets light.

An experiment was done to find out whether all crickets left the cave at one time. They were marked with different colored paint so that the scientists could tell them apart. The first night one third of the crickets went out to find food. They returned at dawn. The next night a different third of the crickets left the cave. One night later the remaining third

CAVE CRICKET

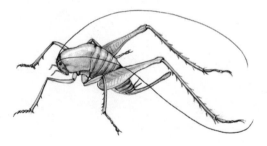

of the crickets left on a food search. The fourth night the cycle repeated. Flies and other insects, such as beetles, feed on the droppings of crickets.

There are more cave beetles than any other cave animals. Once a scientist found many tiny holes on the floors of some caves in Texas. He wondered what made the holes and decided to investigate. After two years of experimenting and observing, the scientist learned the holes were made by a small, quarter-inch long, blind beetle. He discovered the beetle feeds on the eggs of crickets and its whole body seems to be shaped just for that purpose. With its long antennae that have a sense of touch as well as chemical receptors, it taps on the floor of the cave until it finds a hidden cricket egg. Then using its large and powerful mouth parts, or *mandibles,* it clamps onto the eggs and sucks out the insides. The egg is almost as big as the beetle.

CAVE BEETLE

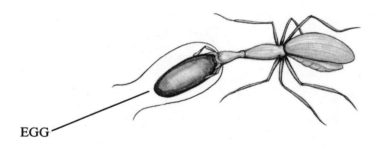

EGG

The guacharo is a bird that lives in caves in South America and Trinidad. Guacharos can fly about in total darkness. Like the bats, they make high pitched click-like sounds that echo back and help them to navigate in the dark. At night guacharos fly out to feed on fruit. When they return they go back to their nests high up in the hollow spaces of the cave.

GUACHARO

## TROGLOPHILES

Troglophiles, such as salamanders and earthworms, are the same animals that are found under things. They like to live where it is dark and cool and are discussed in the following chapter.

# 2 CREATURES THAT LIVE IN

FOWLER TOAD

# THE GROUND AND UNDER THINGS

In a backyard, vacant lot, park, or a farmer's field, or even at the entrance to a cave, there are many things just lying around. A rock, an old log, a piece of cardboard, a battered shoe, a barnboard, an upside-down sled, an automobile tire, or anything that covers the ground might house many tiny animals in the darkness underneath. If anyone bent down to take a closer look, they might be surprised to find animals sticky to touch, long animals, thin animals, furry animals, and animals with dozens of legs.

These small animals stay in the darkness under things for

many reasons. Some want to hide, others like the place for shelter and some need the cool moist earth in order to live. Large animals find the areas an ideal place to find food. They stalk and feed on smaller animals that live there. Others come to mate and lay eggs.

Animals living under things have more food around them. The reason is that right outside their world, next to a rock or near an old log, are green plants, and that means food. More food means more animals.

Because these animals are easy to see and easy to collect and observe, scientists know much more about them than the animals of the cave. Some of these familiar animals are slugs, snails, sow bugs, centipedes, millipedes, earthworms, and ants.

## SLUGS AND SNAILS

A slug looks like a snail that has lost its shell. It is slow-moving, sticky to touch, and about an inch long. It hides under something during the day to stay moist. At night

LAND SLUG

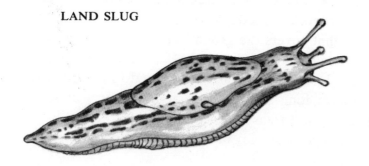

when there is little heat and more moisture in the air it travels. It goes out to feed on tender green plants. If it were caught out in the early morning sun for any length of time, it would quickly dry out and die. It has no protection at all from the hot sun.

A fleshy foot makes up the entire lower side of the slug's body. Along the sides of the foot are openings that secrete a sticky mucus. The slug slides along on this sticky substance about two inches a minute. The mucus is also protective as slugs have crawled over sharp razor blades in experiments and have suffered no harm. When the mucus dries it turns silvery and leaves a trail.

A snail also hides under things. It is a close relative of the slug, and it also does its traveling at night. But if it does not manage to find shelter from the sun during the day, it is protected because it carries its own house. It can seal itself

LAND SNAIL

**25**

inside its shell with its foot. In this way it keeps moisture locked inside, and will not dry out. The snail also withdraws completely inside its shell when attacked.

There are more than 1200 kinds of land snails and slugs in the United States. Most are about an inch long and brownish in color. Their tongues have many tiny teeth that are used to good advantage when eating decaying matter such as leaves and stems of plants often found near fallen logs and rocks.

Snails have right and left spiraled shells. Where the snail's body joins the shell there is a breathing pore. The pore slowly opens and closes. When this happens, air is sucked into the part of the shell covering the snail's lung. Then the air is forced out. All land snails and slugs need air because air contains oxygen that passes into their lungs and allows the animal to breathe. If slugs and snails get water soaked due to spring thaws or rains they move to drier ground where they can breathe.

Both the slug and snail have two pairs of tentacles. The longer pair has eyes on the ends and the shorter pair is used as feelers. The eye stalks move easily and enable a snail to peer over the edge of a leaf. They also lengthen so that the snail can see around a corner. If anyone took a twig and gently touched the end of the eye stalks they would see the eyes and stalk being pulled down into themselves. This is like the finger of a glove being withdrawn.

Snails and slugs are land molluscs. Most molluscs have shells on the outside. Some animals, like a shrimp or crab, can discard their old shells when they are too tight and grow a new one a size larger. Molluscs cannot do this. They carry

26

their houses with them and add on to them as they grow. Land animals extract calcium from rain water to help build these shells and sea animals extract calcium from sea water. Land molluscs have thinner shells since there is less calcium in fresh water than in ocean water.

### SOW BUGS

Other little animals live under things but find their food nearby. Such an animal is the sow bug that is only about a half-inch long. It feeds on live roots and parts of plants that have not decomposed or started to rot. It has a hard armor on top and looks like a miniature army tank. Some species

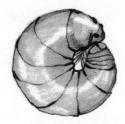

SOW BUG ROLLED IN A BALL

SOW BUG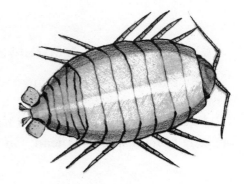

usually protect themselves by rolling up into a ball. When this happens, the sow bug looks like a round ball or pill and that is why it is sometimes called a pill bug; but it is not an insect. It is related to lobsters and crabs. Lobsters and crabs carry moisture on their gills when they are on land, but return to the water often to soak them. Sow bugs do not do this. They carry puddles of water around with them. They gather water from moist soil and store little pools of soil water around their gills.

When their cover is disturbed sow bugs immediately look for new cover. They cannot stay in the sun or their gills will dry out. If the earth under one stone suddenly becomes dry, the sow bugs will crowd together to keep each other moist conserving what little dampness there is. If a sow bug is picked up and put on its back, it immediately will right itself. It does this to protect its gills. The gills are located on the underside and stay wet when the sow bug is right side up.

A few kinds of sow bugs live in their mother's pouch like babies of an opossum and kangaroo. When they are old enough they leave the pouch and look exactly like adult sow bugs.


## CENTIPEDES AND MILLIPEDES

Other animals usually found in darkness under things are centipedes and millipedes.

A centipede is worm-like and has many segments. There are long antennae on the head. On the first body segment is a pair of poison claws. Attached to each segment of the body is one pair of jointed legs. A few kinds have as many as 170 pairs of legs, but 35 pairs is average. A centipede stings and eats insects. In tropical countries the bite of some centipedes is quite poisonous to man.

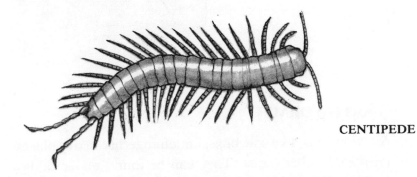

CENTIPEDE

The body of a centipede is flat and long. Due to its long legs it is fast moving and can capture its prey easily. Centipedes usually have more legs than millipedes although centipede means "hundred legger" and millipede means "thousand legger." A millipede has only about 100 pairs of legs. Despite its legs, it is a rather slow-moving animal.

A millipede also has a long body divided into segments. When it is disturbed it curls into a spiral. The head is in the center of the spiral and the animal appears to be dead because it does not move.

The head of a millipede also has antennae. It has a stink gland, too, and this protects it from natural enemies. It does not bite and has no poison glands. Unlike a centipede the millipede does not feed on insects but on fallen leaves found in the forest or meadow.

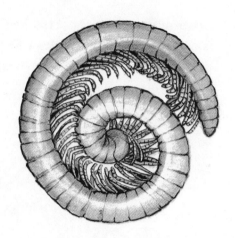

## EARTHWORMS

Earthworms, like sow bugs, bunch together in dry places to keep each other moist. They can be found under things but usually live by the millions in dark, damp soil. Because they prefer darkness and need moisture, earthworms are well-suited to the "underneath" environment.

An earthworm is usually several inches long. It has more than 80 segments, and each has four pairs of bristles called *setae.* These are on or underneath each segment except the

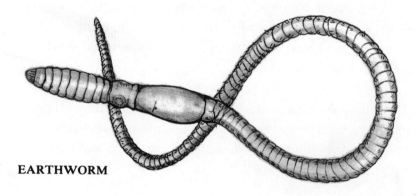

EARTHWORM

30

first and last. The earthworm uses the setae to grasp the earth around it; the body is then pulled forward, one section at a time.

The earthworm can move both forward and backward and if it loses its head because of an accident, it can produce another. Its head houses a nerve cluster that is sensitive to light. The nerve cluster is used to locate the surface of the ground sunlight, which can dry it out.

An earthworm is a great source of food for other animals. It is also valuable in improving the soil. As it crawls through the earth it takes in bits of soil through its mouth. Small particles of food found in the soil are kept by the earthworm and the rest of the soil passes through the body. Much of this soil is deposited on the surface of the ground. As this is done the soil is loosened making it richer and better suited for growing plants.

A slimy substance that the worm spits out helps it to slide through the soil. It does not have lungs but gets oxygen from tiny pockets of air in the soil. The oxygen is absorbed through its moist skin. If the skin dries the worm dies because it no longer can take in oxygen.

If a worm dies, it will most likely be eaten by another animal. One animal that eats dead worms is the ant, which lives under the ground in darkness too.


### ANTS

Ants are known as social insects, which means they live in colonies. Some kinds of ants milk aphids, others cultivate

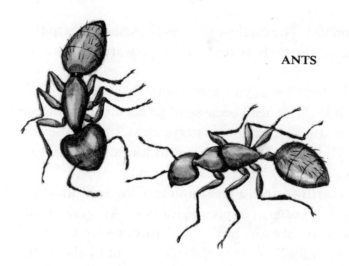

fungi for food and some ants band together and go out on raiding parties to capture "slaves." If a nest is disturbed hundreds of ants carry eggs and pupae to safety through underground tunnels. Other ants in the colony hide in tunnels to protect their queen.

A colony begins when a group of males and one female fly into the air to mate. The males die after the mating. The females, called *queens*, either return to their colony or start a new colony. If it is a new colony, the queen will burrow into the soil or crawl under something and make a burrow. She makes a chamber at the end of the burrow and seals herself inside. Then she lays eggs and licks them clean. She also uses her body to keep them warm.

During the time the eggs grow the queen loses her wings. Also the muscles that were used to power the wings are absorbed into her body and are changed into a liquid food. This food is fed to the first tiny legless *larva* that hatch from the eggs. They look like grains of white rice. As the larvae grow they shed their skin. After several sheddings the larvae form a *pupa.* Inside this pupa the larvae change into adults. This whole changing process in insects is called *metamorphosis.* The small adults are worker ants. They immediately enlarge the nest and feed the queen. They also care for any new eggs the queen lays.

There are 5,000 different kinds of ants. In a single nest there may be as many as 100,000 ants that will demand a diet of 300,000 tiny organisms in a single day.

## NEMATODES

Nematodes are tiny round worms. Some are known as horsehair worms. They are only an inch or so long and can be found most everywhere in soft moist earth. They eat both plants and animals and break down their complex bodies into simpler substances. When this is done other animals can consume the new material and break it down still further.

There are animals that are frequent visitors to dark places under things and they include such animals as moles, shrews, toads, snakes, and salamanders. They visit the underneath world to find food, lay eggs, or to stay in damp, cool places.

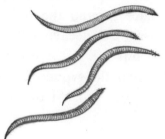

NEMATODES

33

## SALAMANDERS

The red-backed salamander is one animal that looks for food under things and finds earthworms and sow bugs a worthwhile meal. It is rusty colored on top, dark gray on its sides and lighter gray underneath. There are other kinds of salamanders that hide under things, such as the tiger and the spotted salamander.

Salamanders look like lizards but they have no scales like lizards. They are soft-skinned amphibians that can live in water or on land. Salamanders, like their cave relatives, have four legs and a tail. They do not hear well and seem to sense vibrations in the ground with their front legs. They are several inches in length.

Salamanders are cold-blooded, meaning their body temperature is regulated by the surroundings. In the darkness under rocks and logs where the temperature remains fairly constant, salamander body temperatures are also constant.

Land salamanders wander about after dark to search for food. It is done in a slow deliberate way. Usually food comes to them. When an earthworm or sow bug happens to poke its way under a log or rock where there are salamanders, it is snapped up.

In cool climates land salamanders hibernate through the winter. They look for a place around the roots of trees, around a well, under a rotting log or decaying stump, or any place that will remain moist but will not freeze. Sometimes during a particularly cold winter the ground freezes several feet deep and salamanders freeze too. At one time it was

**SPOTTED SALAMANDER**

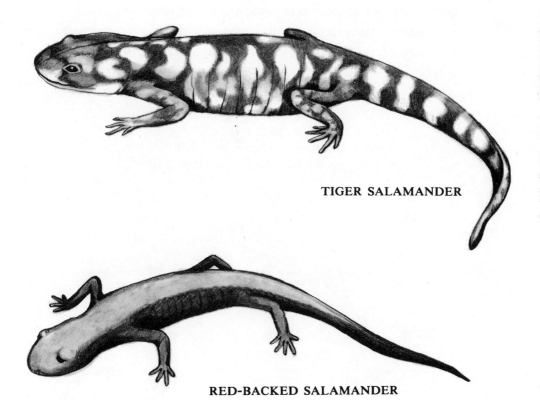

**TIGER SALAMANDER**

**RED-BACKED SALAMANDER**

**35**

believed that salamanders came from fire and could live in flames. Of course this was not true, but most likely the belief began when salamanders were seen wriggling out of a log that had been placed in a fireplace. Because salamanders are often found under the damp bark of logs, it is easy to see that they often ended up in a fireplace with a log.

Young salamanders have the ability to regenerate their limbs. If a salamander loses a limb it can grow a new one. Within ten days, the wound will heal and a stump will form. In four or five weeks the new limb is complete although the color and size are different from the other limbs. Because of this ability to form new limbs scientists study the salamander to find out how this growth takes place. In the future perhaps this knowledge can be applied to man.

## SHREWS

One animal that finds the dark world under a log or rock valuable hunting ground is the shrew. It is only two or three

**SHREW**

inches long but must eat at least once every hour. Because of its constant appetite the underneath world is a favorite territory for the shrew. There it feeds on insects, snails, sowbugs, ants, mice, and even other shrews. It is on the move so much of the day that it wears itself out in a year.

## MOLES

Another animal that hunts under things is the mole. The mole lives underground, tunneling with its spade-like feet and powerful claws. It will often make its way to rocks or

MOLE

logs to look for food. It eats earthworms, insects and other small animals. It digs long burrows just below the surface and roots out grubs with its long nose as it tunnels along. It has soft, fine fur that was once used to make women's coats and capes. It has no external ears and very tiny eyes. Like a shrew it eats most of the time and cannot go more than twelve hours without food.

## TOADS

A toad has been called an ugly prince because, despite its bumpy skin and funny-looking face, it is a most useful animal. It eats any ants, slugs, or caterpillars it can find under a rock or log. The toad is useful to people because it eats such harmful pests as mosquitoes, cutworms, gypsy moth larvae and tent caterpillars.

Its skin may not be much to look at but it is an excellent protection because it disguises the toad from animals that might make a meal of it. The toad usually blends into the background and can only be easily spotted as it hops. When the toad is young it sheds its skin as it grows, sometimes every few days. Toads eat their shedding skin by tugging it toward their mouth as it loosens and then swallowing it.

FOWLER TOAD

There is no truth to the old story that toads cause warts and are poisonous to man. They are not. And since they are easy to tame they make good pets.

## BACTERIA AND PROTOZOA

There are underneath creatures so small they cannot be seen unless a powerful microscope is used. These include the many kinds of bacteria and protozoa. These forms of life are important because they help to decompose leaves, fruit, animal droppings, or dead animals that fall to the ground.

There are hundreds of billions of bacteria in every ounce of soil. They are found everywhere and are so small that several hundred thousand could be placed on the dot of this "i." Bacteria grow best where it is dark, moist, and the temperature is constant; that is why they grow well under things.

BACTERIA

Bacteria are needed for the decaying process. Imagine what a forest would be like if nothing rotted or decayed. Any time a tree died or a leaf fell it would stay on the ground. After years and years the forest would be piled high with dead leaves, plants, and trees. There would be dead animals scattered everywhere. But this does not happen because certain types of bacteria help to break these things down.

Other tiny animals called *protozoa,* animals that consist

of one single cell, can be found under things. Like bacteria they can be seen only through a microscope. They are found almost everywhere though not in as many places as bacteria. In one pound of soil there may be 400 million specimens of these tiny organisms. They play an important role, too, because they help to decay dead plants and animals.

When a tree or plant or animal decays, the energy in it is not lost because the chemicals and minerals it was made of go back into the soil. A plant uses these minerals to manufacture food. Then a slug eats plant leaves. A salamander comes along and eats the slug. Then a garter snake eats the salamander. Later the snake is eaten by a bird. Each animal that is eaten is food by the larger animal. This is an example of a food "chain."

Animals and plants in this small underneath world affect man. Earthworms and ants improve the soil making it better for trees, shrubs, gardens, and crops. The animals and plants

A PROTOZOAN-AMOEBA

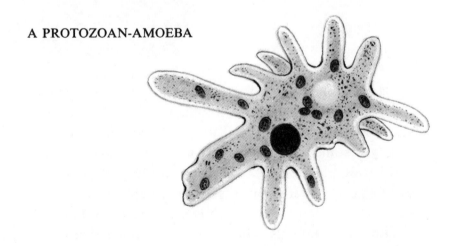

that help the decaying process make it possible to remove dead life from the forest and fields. Underneath animals eat pesky insects in great numbers.

Life under something goes on day after day. Some animals survive and live to the next day. Others become part of the food chain or the decaying process. Either way the energy they have is passed on and on and on.

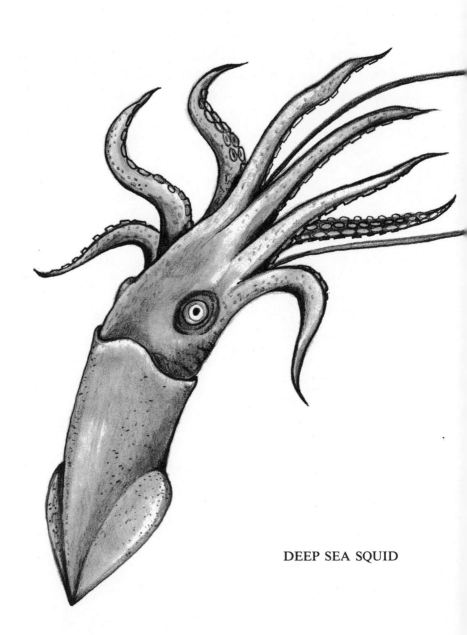

DEEP SEA SQUID

# 3 CREATURES OF THE DEEP SEA

The deep sea is anywhere from 1,000 to 30,000 feet deep, with an average depth of over 12,000 feet—more than two miles.

Creatures that live in the deep sea also live in darkness. There is no sunlight there as the light of the sun does not penetrate more than a few hundred feet at the most. As in a cave, there are no green plants, no changing seasons, no weather, and few sounds when compared to those of the seashore. The water is salty. The temperature is constant—always cold, and there is pressure.

Water pressure is the weight of the water pressing on whatever is underneath it. Anyone lifting a pail of water realizes that water has weight. Seven miles down under the sea the water pressure is three tons per square inch.

Deep sea animals are small, like their cave relatives. Few are greater than several inches in length. Most are smaller than an inch, and of course, some can be seen only with a microscope.

Many of the animals of the deep sea are the same kind as those found in shallow waters. These are sponges, jellyfish, corals, sea fans, and sea anemones, but the deep sea animals, also called animals of the "abyss," are strange looking compared to their shallow water relatives. Very few are brightly-colored. Most are black or are different shades of gray.

All food in the deep sea essentially comes from above. Only green plants can manufacture food, and this takes place only in the presence of sunlight. There are no plants living in the deep sea where there is no light. On the surface of the sea there are tiny floating green plants and animals called *plankton*. The tiny animals feed on the tiny plants. When some of these die, they sink to the sea bottom where they provide food for worms and other small animals. In turn, these animals are eaten by bigger animals of the deep sea.

## SPINY DEEP SEA ANIMALS

Some of the small deep sea animals are starfish, brittle stars, sea urchins, sea lilies, and sea cucumbers. They are all related to each other because they all have spiny skins. The sea cucumber has a leathery skin but there are spines scattered loosely through it.

A starfish does look like a star. The common kinds have five arms, but others can have six, seven, or more. Starfish

STARFISH

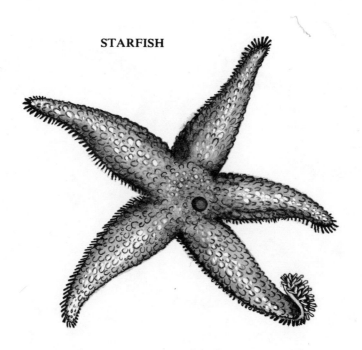

find food by moving along the floor of the sea and "feeling" to find what is good to eat. In shallow seas they only move at a rate of about 15 feet per hour, not very far nor very fast. There is plenty of food for them on the shallow sea floor. But starfish in the abyssal darkness where food is scarce travel more quickly, up to 100 feet per hour.

Brittle stars, a kind of starfish, creep along the sea floor hunting for shrimp and clams and other small animals. Unlike common starfish they do not feel for their food but rely on a super sense of smell. They in turn are eaten by many different kinds of fish.

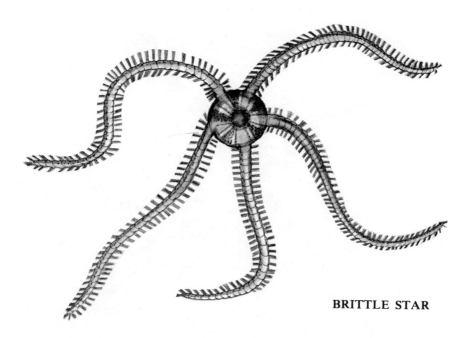

BRITTLE STAR

Sea urchins also live in all parts of the sea. Some of the deep sea kinds have poisonous spines that can injure a man if he just touches one. Scientists who drag nets along the sea floor to find samples of animals must be careful. They wear heavy gloves to keep from being stung after they have raised the nets from hundreds of feet below. Unlike most other deep

SEA URCHIN

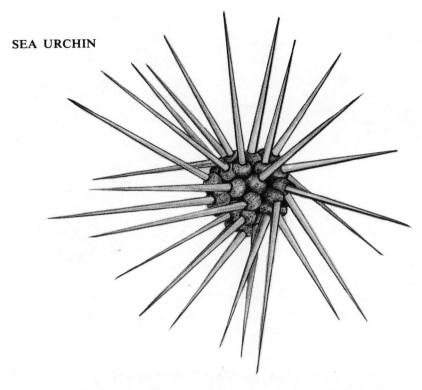

sea animals the largest sea urchins live in the abyss and not in shallow water. One kind is almost a foot across compared to the shallow water sea urchins that are a few inches across. Sea urchins move along the sea bottom feeding on "ooze." They take this mud into their bodies and take out what little nourishment there is; then they spit out what is left.

The deep sea cucumber is a relative of the starfish but it has no spines showing. They are buried in the skin. It plows along like a giant worm on the sea floor swallowing mud and eating the tiny animals that live in the ooze. It also spits out the mud and then takes in more. Some of the deep sea cucumbers have a tail-like tube that sticks up above their

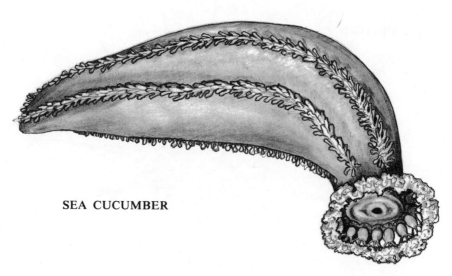

SEA CUCUMBER

bodies. As they push through the mud the tube waves above letting in water. The water contains oxygen that the animal needs to survive.

## SHRIMPS, CRABS AND LOBSTERS

The most numerous of the deep sea animals are shrimps, crabs, and lobsters. Lobsters live on the sea floor, but not in really deep water. They are usually found in water of up to 200 feet deep. Spiny lobsters live in a few feet of water. But there are some deep sea lobsters. A lobster called *Galathea* lives at depths of 500 feet or more and there is a white lobster that lives in water thousands of feet down. Scientists have found a blind lobster they call *Willemoesia* that was brought up from water 12,000 feet deep along the Pacific side of Central America. The adult was only five inches long.

Scientists do not know too much about some deep sea animals. The reason is that they can not get many specimens and those specimens they do get are usually no longer alive. If a net is dragged across the cold bottom of the deep sea and an animal is caught it eventually is raised to warmer surface waters. The animal, used to cold temperatures, may be killed by the warmer water. Or it may be killed by the change in pressure. The animal is used to great pressure. If it is suddenly raised to the surface where water pressure is low it may explode and die suddenly and violently.

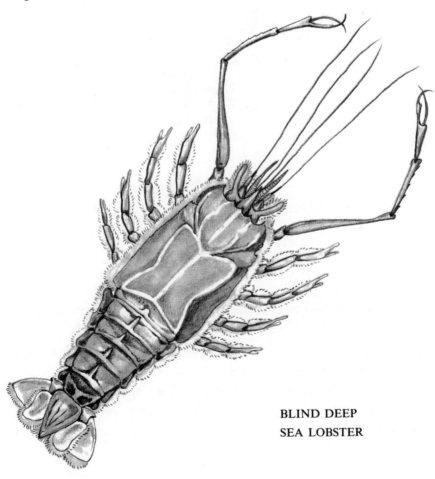

BLIND DEEP
SEA LOBSTER

Shrimp or prawns can survive the change in pressure. A few shrimp have been found 16,000 feet down, more than three miles. Many of the deep sea shrimp have color. Many of them are a brilliant red.

One shrimp, called *Sergestes,* has long antennae which are thin and whip-like, looking similar to a tiny light fishing

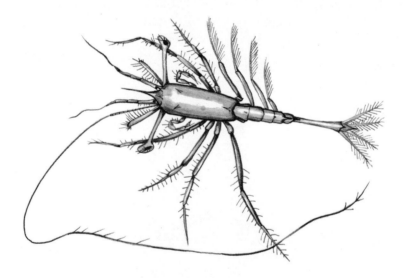

SERGESTES SHRIMP

rod. On the end of the "rod" is an array of "curved hooks." One scientist believes that the hooks are actually used to catch food. When prey is caught on the hook, the shrimp draws it to its legs and the animal is then eaten.

While shrimp do live on the sea floor at the bottom, many live in the darkness of the mid-ocean depths higher up. They stay at a depth of 2,000 feet during the day and then move up to 650 feet at night to feed, moving more than 1,300 feet each day—quite a feat for such small creatures.

There are deep sea hermit crabs as well as other kinds of crabs. The hermit crabs that were dredged up by scientists from the deep sea resembled their relatives of the shallow waters; each had a large abdomen that had to be protected with an empty shell of another sea animal.

One abyssal hermit crab has a luminous sea anemone attached to its body. Scientists think this may be used like a flashlight to light up the darkness around it so that it can see better with its large eyes.

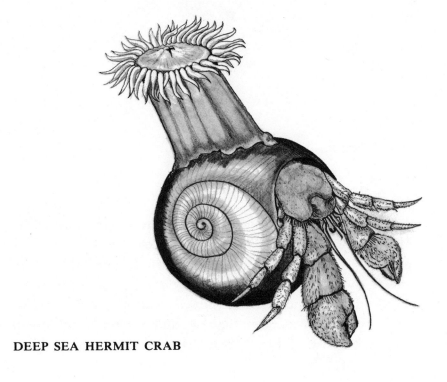

DEEP SEA HERMIT CRAB

LUMINOUS DEEP SEA SQUID

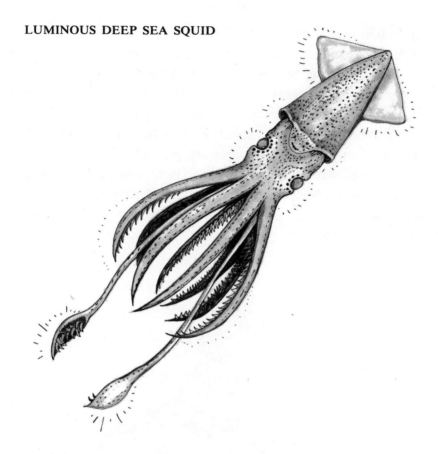

## SQUID AND OCTOPUS

When sailors came back from trips across the seas during
the days of sailing ships they sometimes told of encounters
with giant squid and octopuses that tried to pull their ships
under the water. These huge fiercesome beasts supposedly
lived in the dark chasms of the sea. And if a ship were lost
and never returned, more than one ship's hand on shore said
it was because of the "sea monsters." In actuality, giant

squid are large, over 50 feet including their tentacles, but they are not of such size that they can capture a ship and drag it down into the deep.

Small squid that live on or near the sea floor have weak muscles compared to squid of shallow water. The deep kind also are similar to jellyfish because they are jelly-like and light passes right through their bodies. The insides of the squid can be clearly seen. Some organs, such as the liver, are brightly colored. The squid feed on bits of food and live plankton that drift in the water. Bigger squid feed on fish, small crabs, and shrimp.

These same small deep sea squid are quite different from their shallow water relatives. On the ends of their tentacles are light organs and sharp hooks. Scientists believe that the squid dangles these little lights and that live plankton animals are attracted to the light the same way a moth flies to a lighted window. The hooks are then used to grab plankton. The squid, unlike many sea creatures, never has to travel to find food—it just waits for food to come to it.

There is a blind octopus from the sea floor that is tiny, only about six inches long. It is a fragile animal and looks much like a jellyfish. It is the only known blind octopus in the world. Another deep sea octopus is almost formless and looks like a floor mop.

## FISH

Perhaps the most fascinating animals of the abyss are the fish. These creatures of darkness are constantly searching for food because food is scarce. For this reason a fish must be ready to attack another fish, even if it is larger.

There are several deep sea fish that are called gulpers. The mouth of the gulpers is like a big bag with long teeth and its stomach can expand to hold anything the mouth can swallow. The gulper will grab a fish, even one larger than itself, and hold it in its mouth with its long teeth. Suddenly its mouth will enlarge and it will swallow the big fish, a feat similar to a snake eating a large animal. The gulper is actually drawing its body over the captured fish. Gulpers have a long, whip-like tail that has a reddish light on the end. Scientists think that the gulper uses this light to attract fish in the darkness. When a curious fish moves close to the light, it is quickly gulped inside a giant mouth.

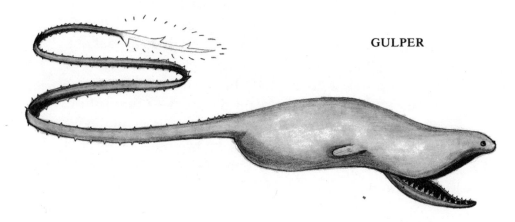

GULPER

Another strange creature of the deep sea is the female angler fish. It is small, about the size of a man's fist. It looks like nothing more than a blubbery ball with a tail, eyes, and huge mouth. But there is something extra. Standing up from

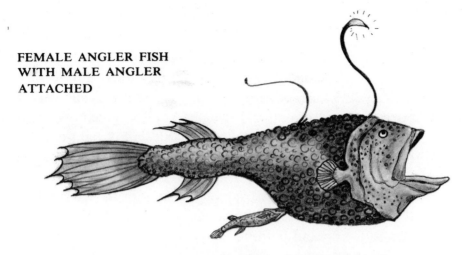

FEMALE ANGLER FISH
WITH MALE ANGLER
ATTACHED

the top of its head is a *barbel,* a piece of flesh that is lit up at the tip. This lit "fishing line" attracts other fish. When they venture too close in the darkness the big mouth of the angler fish snaps them up.

A close relative commonly called the *compleat angler* of the abyss is three inches long and has three hooks on its barbel, as well as a light at the tip. The light attracts other fish and when they are drawn to the compleat angler's mouth, they too become a meal.

Most female angler fish are black or dark brown in color although there is one that is pink. They are ugly. Their skin is covered with warts and bumps and creases. They have small eyes. Male angler fish are much smaller than the female. They are parasites that attach themselves to the female, and obtain nourishment from her body.

There is a great difference in color between deep sea and shallow water fish. In deep water where there is darkness, animals generally have dark colors, unlike the colorless cave animals. They are dark brown or black, although some fish are red and violet.

There is another coloring difference between fish that live on the surface and those that live in the dark. Surface fish are usually silvery or light in color on their bellies and darker on top. The top color is usually blue or green. When a hungry fish looks up it can't see a fish with a light-colored belly since it blends in with the light coming in from the surface. When the bigger and hungry fish looks down on a dark back of a fish, the back blends in with the darkness of the depths. In the deep sea where it is all dark, the fish are one color top and bottom.

Light produced by animals, such as the angler fish, do more than just lure animals close enough to be eaten. The light is also used to see by. Scientists have learned that some fish can emit a light strong enough to send a beam up to two feet forward. One fish, the lantern fish, which looks like a tiny jeweled ship floating in a black velvety mist, has lights that cast a sheet of light downward, enabling it to see the bottom. Also, when the lantern fish swims along the bottom, small animals are attracted to its light. The lantern fish twists around and swallows them up. It uses its light both ways.

LANTERN FISH

Lights are also used as signals in the deep sea. Males and females attract each other during the mating season. A deep sea prawn has some 150 yellow to green lights that flash on and off. One abyssal male fish has a huge light behind its eyes; the female has a smaller light. The much larger female is guided to the male by his bright light. Without these lights it would be most difficult for these animals to find each other.

These lights are also used by deep sea creatures as a form of protection. Sudden lights will confuse an attacker or even blind it for a moment. A fish may be about to grab another fish when it suddenly is confronted with a flash of light. In the darkness it would take several seconds for the eyes of the attacker to become accustomed to the darkness again. In these seconds the fish being attacked could get away. One deep sea shrimp can give off a lighted cloud when it is being attacked. It is like a fiery mist in the water. The attacker sees the cloud of light and by the time the cloud is gone the shrimp is gone, too.

Unlike cave animals, few abyssal animals are blind. We know of a few such as the deep sea octopus and a few fish, but these animals are ones that spend much of their time in the mud on the ocean floor. Scientists believe that most fish with eyes use them to see. Some fish, for example, do not stay in the deep sea all the time. They move to the surface or to a mid-zone, somewhere in between the deep and the surface, where they can use their eyes for feeding and mating.

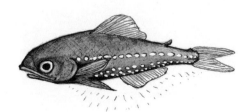 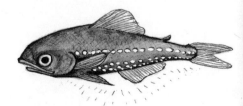

OWL

# 4 NIGHT FLYING CREATURES

At dusk day animals retreat to their nests and dens to bed down for the night. But that is when other animals are just waking up and getting ready to go off into the night to find food or to mate or do both. Many of these creatures are night fliers.

**WOOD MOUSE**

## FIREFLIES

One of these well-known night flying creatures is the firefly, sometimes called the lightning bug. It has its own light just as some of the creatures of the deep sea do. The lights are located on the underside of the belly.

FIREFLIES

Fireflies use their lights to communicate with each other. Males flash their lights which is a signal to females that they are ready to mate. Females flash a light which lets the males know where they are and that they too are ready to mate.

These lights are necessary to mating because there are 40 kinds of fireflies and they flash their lights in different ways and for different time periods. Each kind of firefly can find mates of its own kind by the way it glows.

On rainy nights the larvae of fireflies, called *glowworms,*

**60**

can be seen along the banks of streams and perhaps in a wet ditch alongside a road. On river banks in Thailand whole trees are filled with fireflies. There are so many that when they all glow at the same time the entire tree lights up.

## MOSQUITOES

Perhaps the most annoying night flying insect is the mosquito. Anyone who has been out on a summer night or has camped out in the woods knows all about mosquitoes. The female mosquito bites and leaves a welt that is very itchy. The male mosquito sucks the juices of plants.

Female mosquitoes deposit eggs on the surface of lakes, ponds, and small puddles of water. Even a tiny little puddle in a tin can or in the cup of an acorn can have eggs deposited in it. The eggs stick together looking like miniature rafts

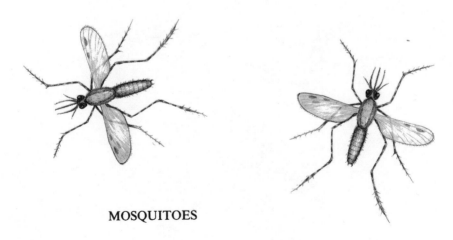

MOSQUITOES

made of black dots. In a few hours the eggs hatch and many wrigglers emerge. This is the larva stage. A wriggler feeds on green algae, tiny plants that grow in water. The wriggler has a long tube for a nose and when it needs a breath of air it sticks its nose above the surface. Inside the tube are tiny hairs that keep out the water. They can breathe only if the water is smooth; that is why female mosquitoes lay eggs in quiet water where there are no waves.

During metamorphosis the wriggler changes from a larva to a pupa and then to an adult. When the wriggler leaves the larva stage its body changes. It grows a wriggly tail and its head becomes very large. It then rests as a pupa. In three days it changes into an adult male or female mosquito and buzzes away. During the day it hides and then appears at dusk to mate and find food.

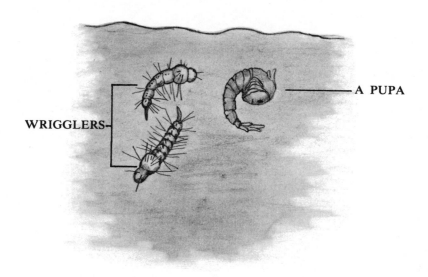

WRIGGLERS—

A PUPA

## MOTHS

Other familiar night flying creatures are moths. They are seen often at the window trying to get in to the light or inside a room flapping around a lampshade.

Some of the moths that flock to the porch light at night are miller moths. If anyone catches one of these moths his or her hand becomes covered with a fine powder sometimes called *miller dust.* This powder is actually wing scales.

A MILLER MOTH

Miller moths are pests and they are the common moths for the adult stages of the corn earworm, army worm, cutworm, and many other pests that destroy plants. Moths lay eggs which hatch into the caterpillars that do the damage.

Some night flying moths are huge, such as the Atlas moth of India that has a ten-inch wing span. Others are tiny, and there is one group of moths that have wing spans less than an eighth of an inch across. The larvae of these tiny caterpillars eat and grow like other caterpillars but spend their entire time between the layers of a leaf!

Moths are well adapted to flying at night. Some kinds have eyes that have little "mirrors" which reflect light the same way as a cat's eye. Some moths are able to find their way in the dark by using the moon in the sky as a guide. The moth flies with the moon kept at a certain angle to its eye. By doing this the moth is able to fly in a straight line. But when the moth comes across a light at night it becomes confused and it begins to circle the light. The moth reacts to this night light as if it were the moon. This causes the moth to circle around and around with each circle getting smaller. Finally the moth touches the light. Moth collectors shine a powerful light on a bright surface such as a white bed sheet and as the moths fly in close, the collectors net the specimens.

Many moths have a good sense of smell in their antennae. The males of one kind of moth can smell the female up to a mile away. Not many adult moths eat or even have mouth parts. But collectors know that adults are attracted by a sweet smell. They can successfully attract moths by putting water and honey in a brightly lit area.

Moths rest during the day. Many look so much like their background that hungry birds cannot find them easily. This is called *camouflage*. The underwing moth, for example, will spend the daylight hours resting on the bark of a tree. It looks very much like the tree bark which makes it difficult for other animals to locate. At night, protected by darkness, these moths can expose their underwings that are a striped red, black, and orange.

Moth caterpillars are also camouflaged. The pesky tomato worm caterpillar is as green as the tomato plant leaves it feeds on. And the sphinx moth caterpillar has green and white stripes that help to blend it in with the pine needles upon which it feeds. Of course the protection does not always work and many caterpillars are eaten by reptiles, insects, amphibians, and birds. Bats also feed on night flying adult moths. Some moths have sensitive hairs on their bodies that tell them when there is movement in the air around them. When they feel the change in the air the moths try to get out of the way of the diving bird or wide winged bat.

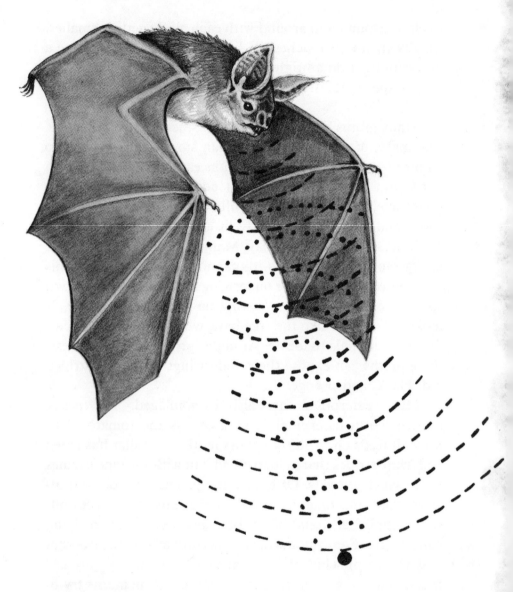

VAMPIRE BAT
WITH SOUND WAVES ECHOING BACK

## BATS

Bats become night flying creatures when outside a cave and they are totally different from the way they act inside a cave. In a cave or attic or church belfry they quietly hang upside down. Outside, they fly through the air and are terrors to the insect world.

Those bats that live in North America eat insects but there are some kinds in Asia and Africa that eat the buds of flowers, and the pollen and nectar of flowers as well as the fruit. They help pollinate plants the same way bees do. A few bats can catch fish and some small bats, called vampire bats, lap the blood from animals.

As a bat flies at night, it avoids bumping into trees and buildings by sending out sound waves through its mouth. When a sound bounces off an object in the dark an echo is picked up by the bat's ears. It is a kind of "sonar" system.

Human ears cannot hear bat sounds which can be sent out at the speed of 250 bursts a second. The bat brain "reads" the sounds as it flies and can determine something just inches away.

However, bats and their sonar are not mistake proof. Bats have been known to run into buildings and trees. Also they may misjudge openings, getting their bodies through but then tearing their wings. They sometimes even misjudge when they swoop down for a drink, and instead of scooping up a drink of water, they get a soaking.

Bats usually catch flying insects with their wings or tail membranes. The wings and tails are curled over and cup shaped when a bat approaches a moth in mid-air. When a moth is captured the bat moves it from the wings or tail to the mouth. The moth wings are snipped off and its wings flutter to the ground while the moth body is devoured.

Female bats usually have just one baby at a time. Northern bats mate in the fall and the babies are born in June or July. When it is time for the baby bat to be born the mother bat hangs rightside up and curls her winged tail upward, making a temporary basket. The baby drops into the basket and then hunts for the mother's nipples to begin nursing on her milk. The eyes open in about nine days.

Baby bats are usually left behind in the caves when the mothers go hunting for insects. But the red bat, among others, carries her baby with her. Eventually the baby gets too heavy and the baby bat is left behind. After about a month the baby no longer nurses and joins the other bats on nighttime excursions.

Perhaps the most misunderstood and most talked about bats are the vampire bats. Books and movies show them as something from the dark ages—huge in size, vicious and ferocious. It is said they suck the blood from victims. However, vampire bats are small, perhaps weighing only an ounce. And while they do live on the blood of animals, they do not usually suck people's blood.

Vampire bats take the blood of such animals as pigs, cows, horses, goats, or others that are usually stabled or fenced in. These bats, found in South America, land on a victim and snip away a bit of the skin with their razor sharp teeth. The horse or cow feels nothing even if it is awake. When the blood oozes out of the wound, the bats lap it up with their tongues. They do not, as so commonly believed, suck the blood with hollow teeth.

For some reason the blood of the victim does not coagulate (get thick) and stop running. Scientists believe it may be some substance in the saliva of the bats that keeps the blood trickling out. The bats can drink blood until they are full but they have never bled any person or any animal to death. People avoid being bitten by the bats by sleeping with a light on or in an area enclosed by screening.

Vampire bats are successful in their feeding because of their small size; it enables them to have a light bite, and then get away very quickly. The little bats may light on their intended victim or land on the ground and hop or walk over to the animal they seek to take blood from. They then find an area of exposed skin, perhaps near the feet or at the ear. When they feed they take in about a tablespoon of blood, quite a huge meal for such a tiny animal.

Sometimes vampire bats transmit rabies, a dreaded disease, to cattle. Other bats can also have rabies and can pass on the disease to humans if a rabid bat bit anyone. Scientists who study bats make sure they handle them very carefully and often they will be vaccinated against rabies beforehand.

### OWLS

Many owls feed at night. Like bats they are often associated with the spookiness of Halloween and mystery stories. But they are not dangerous or spooky creatures.

Generally speaking owls that live in the forests have a territory, or section of the woods that they call their own. It may be a few dozen acres of which the owl knows every single foot. When a baby owl is born it is dependent on its mother and father for about three months. During this time the parents teach the owl chick. The little owl learns its territory by sections. When it has learned the area directly around its nest the parents show it more territory. In three months time it has learned the entire range and is then able to hunt by itself.

When an owl hunts it uses its ears. Its extra sensory ears are most valuable when it looks for a mouse at night. It also uses its huge eyes to see in the dark.

OWL

For years some scientists and naturalists believed that owls could catch a mouse in total darkness. But they were not sure how the owl did it. Finally a scientist experimented with barn owls to see how they caught mice.

The scientist learned that in daylight an owl would spot a mouse on the floor of a huge shed and then swoop down and grasp the mouse with its feet and claws. After the scientist knew how an owl caught its food in the daylight, he watched the owl in complete darkness. The scientist was able to see in the dark using an instrument that shed a beam of infrared light, a light that lets the observer see but not the owl. When a mouse was released on the floor littered with leaves and grass so it resembled a forest floor, the owl caught the mouse each time. When the floor of the shed was changed to sand the mouse escaped because it made very little noise on the sand.

The scientist working on this project realized that owls have a very keen sense of hearing. By using their ears the owls pick up the sounds of living things crawling across the floor of the forest or field. If they are small enough the owls will snatch them up and eat them.

# 5 NOCTURNAL ANIMALS

WHITE-FOOTED MICE

Nighttime also brings out animals that do not fly—creatures that creep, crawl, or run. Mice, raccoons, skunks, and rabbits emerge from their dens or nests. Deer, although seen in the day, do most of their feeding under cover of darkness. Opossums ramble down from tree branches to plod along the ground hunting for wild fruits such as blackberries.

Most nocturnal animals use their eyes to see. They need light but not much. The light of the moon or the faint diffused light from distant stars is enough for them to make their way through the woodland, marsh, or sand dunes to find something to eat. Their eyes may be super sensitive, hundreds of times more adapted to seeing at night than the human eye. They also have good noses and ears plus an excellent sense of touch to help them hunt.

Night accentuates sounds and smells. Air is usually quiet as the winds die down after sunset, and odors can be detected by sharp noses. Sounds that get lost in the bustle of the day can be pinpointed and animals can find their meals by using their ears. Also there is another sense that many night animals have. It is a sense that allows animals to move around in familiar areas without bumping into anything. People can do this. Reaching for a light switch or a doorknob in the dark is often easy for someone who has done the task many times before. When people or animals become familiar with a room or a territory they don't have to see something to know it is there. They remember and can find it even if they are blindfolded. It is called a *kinesthetic sense.*

### FROGS

Night animals also use sound to signal mates. When spring comes, mating sounds drift along on night breezes from bogs, swamps, and marshes. They float through the darkness and anyone familiar with the sounds will listen and say, "The frogs are calling. Spring is finally here."

The earliest night sound we hear in the spring comes from peepers, or tiny tree frogs. They are brown with a dark cross on their backs. They live on plants near ponds and lakes or in the soft wood of rotted tree trunks. Each frog has

SPRING PEEPERS

a large yellow sac on its throat which it puffs out to make the call. After they mate in darkness the females lay eggs in little ponds.

The female hops into the water to lay her eggs one at a time. She hides them in the grasses or under leaves in shallow water. After ten days, tiny tadpoles hatch and wiggle out of the jelly that surrounds them.

## SKUNKS

Another night animal that appears in the spring of the year after spending most of the winter sleeping is the skunk.

STRIPED SKUNK

Skunks stay in a nest or den during the day but come out at night to hunt for food. In fact skunks can suffer greatly in sunlight. Pet skunks have been known to get a nasty sunburn on exposed parts of their bodies around the eyes and paws.

Skunks look for beetles, grubs, or any kind of insect to eat during their night forages. After a hunt on a front lawn at night the green grass is left with small holes, which shows evidence that a skunk has been at work. Many of the grubs eaten by the skunks are harmful to plants so the skunk's food habits are beneficial to man.

A skunk is a handsome animal. It has a bushy tail, and its black fur has one or two white stripes running down the back. Some skunks have spots instead of stripes. Most have pointed noses but there is a hog-nosed skunk that has a snubby face.

Skunks are able to protect themselves very well. When a big, young and foolish dog chases his first skunk he gets sprayed with a liquid that burns and has an unbearable odor. The skunk arches his long tail and squirts the liquid from a sac near its tail. The spray can travel ten feet and when it hits the dog the chase is ended. No dog can stand the smell and sting and it immediately races away. The spray is what makes skunks famous for their smell.


## RACCOONS

Perhaps the most lovable wild animal that hunts food at night is the raccoon. It is also one of the biggest pests because it can turn over rubbish and garbage cans and create tremendous messes in people's backyards. No matter how well a homeowner fastens down the cover of his garbage can, the raccoon can find a way to get it off.

Of course the raccoon does not just spend the night eating garbage. Those raccoons that live near the seashore hunt for crabs and clams and other shelled animals. When they finish their night meal, a neatly stacked pile of shells will be on the beach for an early morning beachcomber to see.

Raccoons that live in the forests and fields eat fruit, frogs, crayfish, and fish. After a hunting trip, the raccoon returns to his den which may be in a hollow tree trunk or in a cozy rock crevice.

RACCOON

In early spring, the mother bears a litter of two to five tiny baby raccoons. She nurses all of them at first. Later she leaves them in the den at night while she hunts for food. Springtime is a busy time for raccoons as they are hungry from the long winter's sleep and the mother must have food not only for herself but for the babies as well.

Raccoons have dark patches under their eyes which makes the raccoon look as though it is wearing a mask. Their fur is soft and long and they have a fluffy tail with rings of light and dark fur. If they are disturbed at night while they sneak onto a back porch to dig into the dog's dish, they will rise on their hind feet and stare. The raccoons will go away and wait until all is clear. Then they will come back to the porch and finish eating. They use their paws like hands to pick up solid food.

## MICE

Various kinds of mice run the fields at night looking for vegetables, grains or other seeds, and nuts. They will also eat all kinds of insects.

Mice nest in an old bird's nest or squirrel nest, or tuck inside an underground tunnel. They may even set up a home in a hollow tree or go inside a warm house and live for the winter. They have been found in cellars, attics, and inside houses that have been closed up for the winter.

Mice that live in the woods only forage at night. They have large eyes and special ear lobes to help them hear during their night wanderings. Despite the protection of the darkness, wood mice are the kind most often caught by owls.

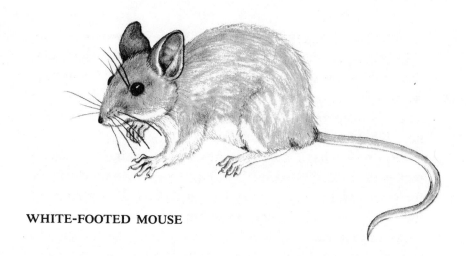

WHITE-FOOTED MOUSE

In a study scientists learned that certain pairs of wood mice are *dominant*, which means they "boss" all the other mice around. When the scientists set traps for mice in the woods they learned that the same pair of mice kept getting caught. The scientists felt that these mice were dominant because they chased all the other mice away and got into the trap first. In other experiments the scientists discovered they were right.

## BADGERS

Badgers also roam the forest floor at night. At first glance a badger might be mistaken for a skunk, but it has white stripes on its face and its tail is not as bushy.

At night, badgers root around the leaves and underbrush looking for insects, but they will also eat mice, lizards, and even gophers and rabbits. They are much more agressive than skunks.

During the day the badger lives in an underground den. With powerful digging claws, the badger digs out a tunnel and nest area and then lines the den with grass and dried leaves.

In winter the badger sleeps most of the time, night and day. On occasion the badger will wake up and go out, especially if it is not too cold. The sleepy animal will look around for some food and then return to its nap.

At night the badger gets along quite well in the darkness because it has a keen sense of smell that helps it locate a meal even though it cannot see it. It also has a highly-developed kinesthetic sense which prevents it from bumping into things.

BADGER

## FLYING SQUIRRELS

Strangely enough one nocturnal animal seems to fly. The flying squirrel uses its sharp eyes and keen ears to glide through the night air. They, unlike bats, do not have real wings and do not really fly. They have loose skin that stretches from the front legs to the rear legs. When the squirrel spreads its legs the skin opens like a kite and the little mammal is able to glide down from its perch in a tree and land on the forest floor.

During the day flying squirrels can be found in a nest in a hollow tree, or they may make a nest in a tree using bits of pieces of bark.

Like ordinary squirrels seen during the day, flying squirrels eat fruits, nuts, and berries. They will also sneak into a bird feeder or dig into a dog's or cat's dish that may have been left out overnight.

FLYING SQUIRREL

# 6 HOW ANIMALS CHANGED TO LIVE IN THE DARK

Creatures of darkness are usually small. There aren't any elephant-sized animals that feed only at night or live where it is dark all the time. Bigger animals need more food, and there just is not an abundance of food under a rock, on the deep sea floor, or inside a cave. Therefore, small creatures of darkness usually require much less food than other animals.

Moles and shrews are exceptions. They use up so much energy that they must eat day and night or they starve. Their system is such that if they go without food for just a few hours they become weak and die.

But most animals that live, mate, or feed in darkness do not need such huge quantities of energy. For example, the slim white salamander of underground Purgatory Creek in Texas has long legs to help it search wide areas for food with little movement. The long legs also help it to keep its head high so it can sense disturbances over a wide area. It also moves slowly and gracefully in the water. This saves energy and does not create currents that would prevent it from detecting food that is nearby.

Animals in dark communities look and live in every possible place to find food. A good example of this occurs in the deep pool of water underground in a place called Squirrel Chimney in northern Florida. Here in this deep pool live two kinds of crayfish. One is the *Procambarus,* which is three to four inches long. The other is the *Troglocambarus,* much smaller, hardly an inch in length. Scientists studied these creatures and determined that they both came from the same ancestor but they adapted differently. The larger crayfish stayed on the bottom of the pool to hunt food. The smaller and lighter crayfish, the Troglocambarus, fed on the ledges of the cave and near the surface of the pool.

Scientists decided that when the little crayfish tried to compete for food with the larger crayfish on the pool floor, the little one lost. The large crayfish got most of the food and those little crayfish that competed with them for food died out in time. The small crayfish that stayed near the top of the pool had it all for themselves. So two kinds of crayfish developed, both living in the same pool but finding food in different places.

We also know that animals of a cave, woodland, or those

**86**

that live in a den can rely on the kinesthetic sense to find their way around in the dark. Many animals have this sense, but it is more highly developed in animals of darkness. For example, the wood mouse can run through dense, tangled undergrowth and turn at high speeds without bumping into anything. It can do this because it knows what is in front of it without actually seeing it. Even though some of these animals have good eyes and ears, or just ordinary eyes and ears, they, at times, have no need for their eyes.

Another generalization that can be made for many animals that live in darkness is that they are long and thin or flat or both. Some animals of the deep sea, like rattail fish, have long tails and are thin. The same is true of animals that live under things such as millipedes or centipedes or earthworms. However, they are shaped this way for different reasons. The rattail is able to withstand the pressure of the ocean bottom more easily by being thin. Millipedes, centipedes, and earthworms can crawl under something or tunnel more easily if they are flat or thin.

Some creatures of darkness have living lights. During the years, animals that had the ability to produce light had advantages. They were able to find their mates in the darkness and they could also find or attract food.

The eyes of some creatures of darkness are very large and have many rods in them. Rods are parts of the eye that make it possible to see in dim light. The tawny owl, a woodland bird, has many rods in its eye. When a mouse runs across the forest floor the tawny owl can see the mouse with only the tiniest glimmer of light available. It would appear to be pitch dark to a human eye.

An owl's eyes would allow it to see sufficiently in a cave, but would the owl be able to catch enough mice to live? Scientists do not think so. Even though the owl could see to catch its prey, it relies heavily on its ears. Inside a cave a mouse would be running over rocks and guano. There would be no rustling leaves giving off sounds. An owl needs to be able to hear its victims as well as see them. What few sounds there were might bounce off rocks in many echoes and the owl would have difficulty tracking down a mouse with these obstacles.

The creatures of darkness that have no eyes usually have very fine senses of hearing, or touch, or taste that enable them to find food.

How did all these special adaptations to living in darkness come about? Charles Darwin, the great English biologist, studied the many ways living things adapted to the conditions in which they live. In general, he believed that those living things that were born with changes favorable to their environment would tend to live or survive. Those that had unfavorable changes would not last and would eventually die out. In this way through the years, animals would change, or *evolve*, and they would become very well adapted to their environment.

In a cave, for example, those animals that were born with larger eyes or better hearing or which were smaller and needed less food would get along better in darkness. They would live longer and have more babies. Those animals that could not find food as well would not live as long and would not produce as many offspring. In time there would be less and less of these animals. Eventually there would be none.

Over millions of years those animals that lived best in darkness would take over the cave or the sea floor or the night air. This process is called *natural selection*.

One thing that everyone can agree on is that creatures of darkness are interesting. They are interesting to observe and study and even much fun to read about. Some creatures of the cave, the deep sea, or the night have lived on this earth for millions of years. As they adapt to new changes it is likely they will be on the earth for millions of years to come.

# BIBLIOGRAPHY

ADULT BOOKS

Idyll, C.P. *Abyss.* New York: T.Y. Crowell, 1964.

Mohr, Charles, E. and Poulson, Thomas L. *The Life of the Cave.* New York: McGraw-Hill Book Co., 1966.

Moore, Ruth. *Evolution.* New York: Life Nature Library, 1962.

Schaller, Friedrich. *Soil Animals.* Ann Arbor: University of Michigan Press, 1968.

## JUVENILE BOOKS

Bronin, Andrew. *The Cave.* New York: Coward, McCann & Geoghegan, 1972.

Callahan, Philip. *Insect Behavior.* New York: Four Winds Press, 1970.

Moore, Shirley. *Biological Clocks and Patterns.* New York: Criterion, 1967.

Palazzo, Tony. *Animals of the Night.* New York: Lion Press, 1970.

Simon, Hilda. *Insect Masquerades.* New York: Viking Press, 1968.

# INDEX

Numbers in italics refer to illustrations.